ARMED LUTHERAN RADIO

YEAR FOUR

+ + +

by Lloyd R Bailey, Jr.

Armed Lutheran Media Company, LLC

First Printing: 2020

Armed Lutheran Media Company, LLC
PO Box 1137
Celina, TX 75009
www.ArmedLutheran.us
ISBN: 978-1-716-39731-8

Send all inquiries to:
armedlutheran@fastmail.com

Published in the United States of America.

All Bible verses are taken from the English Standard Version (ESV). References to Luther's Works (LW) are taken from the American Edition.

CONTENTS

DEDICATION

This book is dedicated to my beautiful wife Tammy

For her constant support and inspiration.

Thank you for being my biggest cheerleader.

And to my wonderful children Reagan and Rylyn.

Thank you for your constant love and support.

PREFACE

This book is my fourth collection of commentaries on life as a Christian gun owner, observations on the culture, the nature of freedom, and the origin of our rights. The chapters that follow are adapted from my show notes from the 51 episodes that we produced in 2019.

All have been revisited and revised to make the lessons and insights more timeless and to focus less on specific events or people. Some have been completely re-written because my original notes were just awful, quite frankly.

I hope you enjoy the book and learn something along the way.

Thank you to the listeners who download and listened to Armed Lutheran Radio each week. And a special thank you to listeners who became members of the Reformation Gun Club. From the bottom of my heart, thank you for your support!

PRAYING THE TEN COMMANDMENTS

How many people have you heard talk about a major decision in their lives — about a job change, a move, a career change, family decisions, health decisions — and they say "I prayed about it" and decided what's best?

Have *you* done that?

When you think of the 10 Commandments, what comes to mind? Rules? Restrictions? Laws?

Martin Luther encouraged people to look at important texts, like the Ten Commandments, in different ways. He wrote a book on prayer for his barber — a man named Peter — and put forward a simple method for praying texts like the Commandments, the Apostles' Creed, etc.[1]

In this letter, Luther breaks each commandment down into four parts: instruction, thanksgiving, confession, and prayer.

---

[1] Luther's Works, Volume 43, 193-211. See also "A Simple Way to Pray," available on Amazon or at CPH.

First, we ask ourselves what God demands of us.

Second, we thank God "for placing around us the protection of the law."

Third, "We recognize the ways we have sinned against the commandments."

And fourth, "We pray that the Lord helps us understand his commandments," and "to resist the temptation to violate them."

Mainstream America — the political Left, our media, our celebrities, and politicians (sorry that was redundant) — have largely rejected Christianity and its values and teachings. And we see the tragic results every day.

They say we need to change man-made laws to restrict people's freedoms so they will be unable to commit crimes against one another. But what we really need is a recognition of two things: God's law, and our inclination to sin.[2]

---

2 Also called "concupiscence."

When you face major decisions in your life, pray the Ten Commandments and apply them to your own situation.

Maybe it's a job change, a financial investment, a personal relationship (especially one of a romantic nature), or a plot to take over the world. Whatever it might be, praying the Ten Commandments will lead you to better decisions.

As you will no doubt see in the following chapters, the Ten Commandments can clearly be applied to stories of crime, self-defense, and politics. A great deal of pain, heartache, and suffering could be avoided if more people recognized this fact and applied this technique in their own lives.

THE BEST A MAN CAN GET

The big brouhaha on Super Bowl Sunday in 2019 was an advertisement by Gillette calling on men to be the best they can be. How? By removing your testicles and bowing at the altar of woke feminism.

The ad insinuates that masculinity — that MEN — are just plain bad, and need to be better. Some men are not bad it says, but *most* need to be better.

Most.

Predictably, the conservative social media universe exploded with calls for boycotts and the burning of overpriced Gillette products.

But the truth is that men *do* need to be better. But not the way Gillette and the pussy hat-wearing feminists think. We need the kind of masculinity that stands up for the weak, protects children, defends the chastity and honor of women, and sets an example for young men to follow by serving as faithful husbands and fathers.

We have a perfect example to follow. It is in the Bible.

Consider Luther's explanation of the Sixth Commandment:

> *"We should fear and love God that we may lead a chaste and decent life in words and deeds, and each love and honor his spouse."*

Joseph, the Earthly father of Christ, is a perfect role model for men. He took the difficult path to protect his wife's reputation when she was found with child.[3] He packed up his family and fled to Egypt to protect them from harm and then brought them back to Israel when it was safe.[4]

But society has shunned *that* kind of masculinity. It has turned from virtue and morality based on Biblical truth and seeks virtue in places where virtue does not exist. When the going gets tough, the modern Joseph gets going somewhere

---

3 Matthew 1:18-25

4 Matthew 2:13-23

else, leaving their Marys to raise their children alone (or with a series of boyfriends or step-fathers).

Making things worse, the modern feminist movement suggests that men are scoundrels who just need to be taught not to be rapists.

Modern society fails — as all of liberalism fails — to recognize that men (and women) are sinners. We all sin and fall short of the glory of God. Biblical virtue, morality based on God's word, calls us to be better than we are. The best a man can get.

Society has shunned God's word, so with no shared sense of virtue, with no shared values, what do men aspire to be? How do they measure themselves? They measure themselves based on their own opinions and desires.

And, inevitably, they fall.

Modern feminism only cares about women who vote for progressive candidates and who support progressive policies.

If you support traditional marriage, traditional gender roles, if you oppose abortion, if you're a stay-at-home mom, if you're a home-school mom, the Left doesn't consider you a woman at all.

As long as our society continues to reject God's design for men and women and the nuclear family, we will be forced to endure meaningless virtue-signaling, brought to us by corporations who on the one hand tell us to be better men, to treat women better, while at the same time objectifying

women by plastering their company logos on skin-tight leather jumpsuits worn by curvy women at car races.

So, remember the Sixth Commandment. Hold fast to your wives. Honor and cherish them. Shave however you like.

Just don't get bent out of shape by silly commercials.

A DEADLY POLICE RAID

Calling gun violence one of the 'greatest public health epidemics facing the nation,' Houston Police Chief Art Acevedo testified before Congress in support of new gun control.

*"Acevedo pressed Congress…to pass a 'red flag' law and tighten background check requirements this year, adding that **saving one life is enough to justify new restrictions**.*

Amid what he referred to as 'almost regular mass shootings' in the United States, Acevedo asked lawmakers to use common sense to balance Second Amendment protections while addressing gun violence. He then implored lawmakers to 'act now' to require universal background checks, expand mental health services and pass 'red flag' provisions to temporarily take guns from people deemed by a judge to present a danger to themselves or others.

I will discuss the shooting of those police officers in a moment. But first, let's consider what this is. This is a public official — the Police Chief of Houston — calling on Congress to move to restrict the rights of law-abiding citizens. He is entitled to his opinions about gun violence, but he's not entitled to his own facts.

Romans 13 lays out the blueprint for our submission to authority, the authority granted by God to people like Chief Acevedo. He is entrusted, by the people, to uphold the Constitution and to "protect and serve," correct? Restricting the human rights of millions to save just one life (assuming that would even be possible) is not what God has entrusted the chief to do.

---

[5] https://www.chron.com/news/article/acevedo-to-congress-on-gun-control-doing-13594630.php

The failure to recognize and address the root causes of violence — namely sin — leads the godless Left to push for heavy-handed, illogical government solutions. Limiting the freedoms of law-abiding citizens to claim that you've done something about crime. All you are doing is disarming the people who are not the problem.

Fifteen to twenty years ago, when drunk driving was a hot topic, there was a public safety campaign to reduce drunk driving deaths. And those deaths have declined year over year. How? By making it harder for people to buy alcohol? By making it harder to use recreational drugs? No. Both of those things arc as readily available as ever and even more so in some places as blue laws have been reversed and Marijuana has been legalized.

Did we make it harder for people who don't drink to buy a car? No.

So why do we approach the "gun violence" issue this way?

This is scapegoating. Blaming law-abiding gun owners, the NRA, and politicians who don't go along with the gun control agenda, for causing the blood in the streets and the tears of victims.

Now, to that previously mentioned incident where five Houston police officers were shot during a drug raid. This incident was cited by Chief Acevedo to underscore the need for gun control. There's just one small problem with that, however. Well, more than one problem, actually. The facts of the case disprove his claims and actually underscore the need for greater scrutiny of police tactics and procedures.

Officers launched a "no-knock" raid based on an anonymous tip and the word of a confidential informant. The informant claimed he had bought black tar heroin from the homeowner. There was no surveillance. No in-depth investigation. No undercover operation. Just a tip from someone who is most likely a drug dealer or former drug dealer himself.

And so, based on this clearly unimpeachable source, five narcotics officers in plain clothes kicked in the door of that home one evening and a gunfight erupted. The homeowner, probably believing he was the target of a home invasion, opened fire, wounding five officers. The homeowner, his wife, and his dog were all dead when the dust had settled.

As rumors spread that this was a botched raid and that the homeowners were innocent, Joe Gamaldi, President of the Houston Police Officers Union held an angry press conference where he chided citizens who were critical of the police and their actions.

> *"We are sick and tired of having targets on our back. We are sick and tired of having **dirtbags** trying to take our lives when all we're trying to do is protect this community and protect our families. Enough is enough."*[6]

Gamaldi angrily suggested that they would be keeping track of people who were critical of the police actions in this raid.

---

6 https://reason.com/archives/2019/02/06/one-deadly-drug-raid-and-two-red-herring

Chief Acevedo later distanced himself from the comments and said Gamaldi misspoke but went on to say more needs to be done to keep guns out of the hands of people who should not have them. He again called for more background checks, a reinstatement of the Clinton Assault Weapons Ban, and a magazine capacity ban.

So, who were these "dirtbags" Mr. Gamaldi was referring to? Dennis Tuttle and Rhogena Nicholas. They had lived in that house for over 20 years. They had no criminal records. Tuttle was an honorably discharged Marine veteran. Rhogena was a cancer survivor.

Neighbors described the couple as good people, wonderful friends. One woman said she and Rhogena were very close because they were both fighting cancer and they spoke daily she said.

Doesn't sound like "dirtbags" to me.

Naturally, none of the officers in the raid wore a body camera, so all we have to go on is the word of the police which, as it turns out, isn't worth much. According to reports, the first cop through the door killed the couple's dog with a shotgun. Tuttle then returned fire wounding one of the intruders. Nicholas attempted to disarm the wounded officer and then she was shot and killed. Tuttle was then killed.

Guess what the police found when they searched the house. Not a damn thing. A revolver and a couple of shotguns. Tuttle had been armed with the revolver.

And not a single drop of black tar heroin. Not even one.

So, Houston Police mounted a no-knock raid based on the word of a criminal, they stormed into the couple's house, shot their dog, and when the homeowner returned fire, they killed him and his wife.

And then they found nothing to substantiate the claims of the informant. And when the public questioned their actions, the Police Union referred to the dead homeowners as "dirtbags," and the Police Chief used the botched raid to call for more gun control.

I did not know this at the time but it turned out that the officers lied to obtain the search warrant. As I suspected at the time, the whole thing was the result of dirty cops, not drugs or guns. The "dirtbags" were wearing badges.

As of this writing Chief Acevedo is still advocating for more gun control, Joe Gamaldi never apologized for his cruel slander, and Dennis Tuttle and Rhogena Nicholas are still dead. To my knowledge, their families have not been compensated for their wrongful deaths.

Consider the explanation of the Eighth Commandment from the Small Catechism:

> *"We should fear and love God that we may not deceitfully belie, betray, slander, or defame our neighbor, but defend him, [think and] speak well of him, and put the best construction on everything."[7]*

The police have a responsibility to put the best construction on the evidence they receive. They should work to corroborate the reports before mounting an armed raid. In

---

[7] The Small Catechism of Martin Luther

this case, the officers who requested the search warrant intentionally lied. The police union president referred to the victims as "dirtbags" and threatened to surveil anyone who dared criticize the raid. And then the police chief falsely used this tragedy to suggest that anyone who opposes gun control is responsible for blood in the streets and the tears of the families of the victims of violence. What about the tears of the families of unlawful police violence?

Consider the Fifth Commandment, as well. It also applies to the policy of no-knock search warrants.

> *"We should fear and love God that we may not hurt nor harm our neighbor in his body, but help and befriend him in every bodily need [in every need and danger of life and body]."*[8]

High-risk armed raids are inherently a danger to the officers and the targets. If things go perfectly, everyone goes home safe and the bad guy goes to jail. If not, police officers are injured or killed. In the worst possible case, innocent citizens are killed. In this case, the victims were murdered by agents

---

[8] ibid

of the state.

Setting aside the deceit of the dirty cops, this was a violent assault against a suburban couple who were alleged to be selling drugs, not violent gang-bangers. Our lawmakers and law enforcement officials should consider the Fifth Commandment carefully concerning the policy of no-knock raids against non-violent suspects. Is the end goal — arresting an alleged drug dealer — worth the risk of losing the lives of police officers and or civilians? I don't think so.

Nothing Chief Acevedo supports would have prevented the shooting of his officers. The couple had no criminal record so

they were not prohibited from owning guns. They did not have an "assault weapon," unless you consider a six-shot revolver an assault weapon. So nothing the chief prescribes would have prevented this.

Do you think this could happen again? You bet. As long as the law allows this kind of tactic — based on flimsy evidence and the word of dirty cops — any one of us could be targeted by an anonymous tip from someone with a grudge.

Senator Rand Paul of Kentucky has proposed a law to outlaw no-knock raids. To use Chief Acevedo's logic against him, if it saves one innocent life, it's worth it.

And finally, when politicians glibly talk about gun confiscation and going door-to-door, it's easy to laugh that off and think that it's an absurd idea. Police officers would not willingly go along with such a policy. They would never kick in the doors of innocent people!

Many would not. But we have enough evidence to prove that some would. And even one is too many.

CHRISTCHURCH

A 28-year-old racist, Neo-Fascist — whose name shall not be mentioned — walked into two Mosques in Christchurch, New Zealand on March 15, 2019, and opened fire on worshipers. When he was finally taken into custody 51 were dead and 40 more had been injured.

Before the attack he released a manifesto saying that part of his goal in this attack was to ignite a "race war." How original.

The shooter live-streamed the attack using body-cameras. The whole thing played out in gruesome detail like some violent video games, live on the internet. But the victims were not digital avatars representing real gamers, they were real. Their pain, and blood, and deaths were real.

We've often talked about the strange contradiction that is the internet. How it connects us in ways never before dreamed of, and yet we are more disconnected from each other than ever before.

The evil that visited the mosques in Christchurch has a home in the bowels of the internet. Where people who feel

alienated, angry, and confused, can find purpose, meaning, and allies. Their internet presence gives their empty lives meaning. It validates their ugliest beliefs.

The shooter complained in his manifesto about the degradation of Western culture. The answer to a world without meaning or hope is not to be found on the internet, or in our culture or politics. Western Culture, and the values it instills, is not defended through mass murder.

Our hope rests on Christ and His promises. Those values still exist, and ever shall, in the word of God.

It is easy to become despondent and angry about the way of the world around us. The sexual revolution and the damage it has done. The culture of violence we have created and celebrate. The murder of 40 million unborn children each year around the world in the name of "women's rights." The hedonism of the West that the fundamentalists of the East rail against.

Like the killers of ISIS or Al Qaeda, the killer in New Zealand convinced himself that the solution to the world's moral failings is murder.

All that will do is further the decline into the abyss.

The answers are in our hands. Aside from a few places, like China and North Korea, access to the word of God is available for all. It is the hope and promise of a new life beyond this veil of tears. It is why the greatest growth in the church is in Africa and Asia, not in the west. Those who grow up in war and famine and strife cling to the promise of something greater.

They recognize, as we would do well to remember, that this is not our home.

Dear Christian, as we look forward to Easter on our Lenten journey of reflection and repentance, we can see the promise of forgiveness and eternal life. In Jesus. On the cross. In the tomb. Descended into hell. Raised again from the dead. Paying the ransom for our sins.

Our weapons in this fight are not of this world. We stand on the solid rock of God's word. Not on the shifting sands of our decaying culture.

I hope you will join me in praying for the dead and injured and for their families and for the city of Christchurch.

And in praying for the shooter, that he may recognize his own sin and come to repentance.

AS I SEE IT

I shared a link to episode 163 in a certain Christian social media group, of which I am a member. It is a closed group and one of the stipulations is that we don't share posts or discussions outside of the group. So, out of respect for the group, I will not mention it or any of its members by name.

In response to my post, another member — whom we will simply call "Fred" — asked the administrators to remove my post because he claimed that I was violating the Eighth Commandment by referring to "anti-gun Christians" or "gun banners."

So, I want to address the question of the Eighth Commandment and how it applies here, and why it's important to name things according to what they are and what they believe.

So, what is the Eighth Commandment?

"Thou shalt not bear false witness against thy neighbor."

So, false witness…like false testimony in court? Yes, but there is much more to it than that.

Remember, as Lutherans, we apply the Ten Commandments more broadly. They are not just a bunch of "thou shall nots." There's more to each of them and part of the Christian life is about applying the Commandments to your decisions and your actions as I discussed in the previous chapter.

The Commandments really boil down to two fundamental concepts. (1) Love of God and (2) love of neighbor. With respect to the Eighth commandment, it is about loving your neighbor so that you do not harm his reputation or good name.

In Luther's explanation of the Eighth commandment in the small catechism we read:

> *"We should fear and love God that we may not deceitfully belie, betray, slander, or defame our neighbor, but defend him, [think and] speak well of him, and put the best construction on everything."*[9]

---

[9] ibid

So, what we are talking about here is the slandering and defaming part. And, according to my critic "Fred," the deceitful part.

Here's what Fred had to say initially. I'm going to paraphrase rather than quote him directly. His first two points were that (a) he did not know of any Christians who want to ban guns, and (b) using the term "anti-gun" is misleading and is no different than when the LGBTQ crowd calls us "anti-gay."

So, let's dig into these claims.

"There are no Anti-Gun Christians"

First, let's address this claim that there are no Christians who want to ban guns.

As we have discussed at length on the podcast, there are entire church bodies who make it quite clear — in their resolutions, their constitutions, their official statements — that they oppose the ownership of firearms. Any firearms.

Specifically, let's look at the Evangelical Lutheran Churches in America (ELCA), the Presbyterian Church USA (PC-USA), and the United Methodist Church (UMC). These churches, and many others, have written positions on gun violence, which all say essentially the same thing. They ignore the issue of sin (or they gloss over it) and focus almost exclusively on guns.

On the website for the UMC (the church that I grew up in, by the way) they have a statement on what they call "gun violence."[10]

That statement is based on a really bad interpretation of Micah 4:1-4, where the people of God, after his return, will beat their swords into plowshares. This is a prophetic vision of what will happen *after* God returns, not a condition that is required *before* His return, as the UMC seems to think.

Of the eight ways they suggest that United Methodists can get involved to reduce gun violence, they suggest that congregations advocate for "Universal Background Checks," and a ban on private sales and transfers of firearms. This is a call to criminalize the sale of private property without an

---

10 http://www.umc.org/what-we-believe/does-the-united-methodist-church-have-a-position-on-gun-control

intermediary (i.e.: big government).The Presbyterian Church USA supports the outright **ban** of semiautomatic rifles. They are not talking about automatic weapons. They want to **ban** rifles like my son's .22 caliber Ruger 10/22 or the Marlin 60 that I was given as a child. They want the government to **ban** certain kinds of guns that they don't like but know next to nothing about.[11]

They care so much about saving lives that they also overwhelmingly oppose any consideration of abortion restrictions. But, I digress…

The UMC, PC USA, and the ELCA all support laws **banning** the sale of "assault weapons" and the sale of "high capacity" magazines. They do not define what those are, but this is a call to ban the ownership of property that is legally owned by people who are not criminals. (Not yet, anyway.)

Then there are Evangelical "pastors" like Rob Schenck and John Piper (to name just two), who make it clear that they oppose the idea of gun ownership, especially for self-defense.

---

[11] https://www.pcusa.org/news/2014/6/19/assembly-acts-decisively-gun-violence-abortion-tax/

We have heard from people like ELCA Lutheran pastor Mark Knutsen who, from the pulpit of his Church in Eugene Oregon, calls for new laws to **ban and confiscate** firearms from law-abiding citizens. Not from criminals. From innocent Oregonians whose firearms are not used in a crime.

So, as I pointed out to "Fred," there are plenty of Christians

who explicitly call for banning guns. And a good many of them do it from the pulpit. If you doubt that claim, go listen to the first three years of Armed Lutheran Radio and our Clinging to God and Guns segments.

If "Fred" doesn't know any Christians who are anti-gun, clearly he doesn't get out much.

"Anti-Gun equals Anti-Gay"

Now, let's take a look at Fred's second claim, that calling someone anti-gun is the same as calling a conservative Christian "anti-gay." Is it fair to say that labeling someone as "anti-gun" who wants to ban *some* guns is the same as calling them "anti-gay" if they support the Biblical view of marriage?

Those who oppose gay marriage or who support the traditional, Biblical view of marriage, don't want to criminalize or ban gay people. They do not want to enforce outdated sodomy laws or hang gays in the public square like they do in Muslim countries. They simply oppose the redefinition of God's institution of marriage to include unions which God clearly condemns. They recognize that to devalue and re-define what it means to be married is to undermine the family, which used to be the foundation of our civilization.

Unlike the gun-banners, they do not want to put gay people in jail. They do not want to make simply *being gay* a crime. Those who seek to ban guns want to re-define what "assault weapon" means in order to mislead people and to turn innocent people into criminals. They hate guns and want to ban them.

Christians who oppose gun ownership do so because they hate guns and they want gun owners sent to prison if they do not comply.

Christians who oppose gay marriage do not do so because they hate gays. They do not want to see them sent to prison for simply being gay. So to call them "anti-gay" is an Eighth Commandment insult.

Those who call conservative Christians "anti-gay" are doing so to silence speech that they don't like. They do it in the hopes of shaming us into silence. They want to frame us as "haters" and to suggest that we *hate* gay people.

That's very different from wanting to ban and confiscate the private property of millions of Americans and to turn them into criminals for refusing to surrender to the government property that they purchased legally. It's not the same as

wanting to criminalize the transfer of a firearm to a friend or family member without first asking Daddy Government for permission.

That **is** the very definition of "anti-gun." Either you support gun rights or you do not. It is really that simple.

Saying that you want to ban *certain kinds* of guns that you don't like while claiming that you are not "anti-gun," is a bit like saying you only want to criminalize *some* homosexual acts, but not all of them.

The Eighth Commandment

As my conversation with "Fred" wore on, I began to suspect that he was really offended by my support for gun rights and not by my use of the supposedly offensive adjectives. And, sure enough, I was right.

Ultimately he accused me of crafting my words in a deceptive way and, for good measure, he decided to call me a "troll" and to refer to my opinion as "bile."

So, while accusing me of violating the Eighth Commandment, he violated the Eighth commandment himself by impugning my motives and resorting to *ad hominem* attacks. Projection much?

Let's ignore Fred's insults and sum up his underlying point.

Is it misleading to call someone "anti-gun" who wants to ban so-called "assault weapons," for example? Is it unfair to suggest that they want to ban *all* guns when they only refer to banning a specific type of gun?

I suspect there are a number of well-meaning people who are in this position, mainly because they are ill-informed on the issue. They don't oppose guns *per se*, they just don't like the ones that look scary. They have bought into the media-driven nonsense about "assault rifles."

Perhaps they equate gun ownership with hunting rifles or shotguns, not weapons for self-defense.[12]

Is it dishonest or misleading to refer to these people as "gun banners" or "anti-gun?" People, who just want to stop innocent people from dying but shortsightedly believe that legal ownership of certain kinds of guns are the problem?

No, it is not.

Words mean things. If you want to ban guns — any guns —

you are by definition a "gun-banner." There's no need to distinguish those who want to ban *some* guns from those who want to ban *all* guns.

---

12 We call these people "Fudds," as in Elmer Fudd.

When we use these terms, we use them to describe, briefly, the kinds of people we are dealing with and the ideas that they support.

It is like calling Joel Osteen or Joyce Meyer a heretic or Creflo Dollar a "prosperity preacher."

When someone supports abortion on demand, just not partial-birth abortion, we don't violate the Eighth commandment by calling them "pro-abortion." We don't twist ourselves into pretzels to call them "almost pro-life" or "sort-of pro-abortion."

There is a parallel to views on the infallibility of Scripture. Either you believe the Bible — all of it — or you have no basis to defend any of it. If you believe one verse or chapter is false, how do you then say with any authority that another verse or chapter is absolute truth? You cannot.

If you oppose the legal ownership of one type of firearm, how do you then say with any conviction that another type is permissible? If one type must be banned because they are too dangerous, can't you then conclude that all types of guns must be banned for the same reason?

In the same way that you cannot call someone a "Bible-believing Christian" who does not accept the infallibility of Scripture, you cannot claim that someone is "pro-gun" who wants to ban guns of any type. If you want to ban guns — any guns, or all of them — you are a "gun banner." Pure and simple.

And the fact that people like "Fred" got their jimmies rustled about it, says more about "Fred" than it does about me or the Eighth commandment.

I'm just calling it as I see it.

EASTER 2019

Today is Easter. And this past weekend was the Arkansas State IDPA Championship in Perryville Arkansas. What does that have to do with Easter, you ask?

If you follow my other podcast, *Unload and Show Clear*, you saw my live videos from the Arkansas match and you saw how miserable the weather was. It was rainy, 52 degrees, windy, and cold. By the end of the match, I was soaked through. I could not feel my fingers. I could not hold onto the gun. I could not get warm. I resorted to making a poncho out of a trash bag, but it did not help.

It was absolutely miserable.

This past Friday night I took my kids with me to church for the Good Friday Tenebrae service. For those unaccustomed to orthodox Christian services, Tenebrae services feature a gradual extinguishing of the candles on the altar, finishing with a *strepitus*,[13] a loud noise taking place in total darkness at the end of the service.

This is a recreation of the final moments of Christ's passion, as he gave up his spirit and the earth quaked, the sky went black, and the veil in the temple split in two.

I was reminded in that service, as we reflected on the suffering of our Savior, that whatever misery and suffering we experience in our lives, it pales in comparison to Christ's passion.

The shivering and cold, the stiff fingers, the joint pain many of us felt while standing in the rain that weekend in Arkansas was nothing when compared to the bitter pain, the betrayal, the physical and mental anguish suffered by Jesus on the cross as he took the sins of the world — past, present, and future — onto himself. He became sin himself so that we might be justified before Holy God on the last day.

We face many trials in our own lives. The deaths of friends and loved ones. The loss of a child. Economic hardship.

---

[13] Latin, meaning "loud noise"

Poverty. Addiction. Disease. Injuries. Bad weather which damages our homes, our vehicles, our crops. Or which leaves us shivering, wet and cold at an event that we should be enjoying.

During those times it may be tempting to blame God. To ask Him why. "Why me, Lord?" And that's okay. It is human nature.

Is that a sin? Yeah. But don't worry. Jesus paid for *that* sin, too.

Remember, Jesus never promised us our "best lives now," as the prosperity preachers might tell you. He never promised us peace, health, wealth, or abundance.

He promised that all who have faith in him might have eternal life. He promised that though we may suffer in this world, we who put our faith in His promises will live eternally in the next.

Happy Easter. He is risen! He is risen, indeed! Hallelujah!

RILEY HOWELL

We heard again at the National Rifle Association's Annual Meetings, from people like President Donald Trump and others, the mantra that "the only thing that stops a bad guy with a gun is a good guy with a gun." That tired, worn-out slogan was first uttered by NRA Executive Vice-President Wayne LaPierre after the Newtown school shooting.

I really wish people would just stop. While a gun may make it easier, plenty of good guys with guns have lost their fights with bad guys. Just watch John Correia's videos on the Active Self Protection YouTube channel if you want to see it happen.

The real truth is that the only thing that will stop a bad guy with a gun is a good guy with the will and determination to fight back whether they have a gun or not.

On April 30, 2019, a gunman at the University of North Carolina at Charlotte (UNCC), killed two other students and wounded four more. This shooting hit home for my family.

My wife is a UNCC alumnus. We follow the school's sports teams. We go to their basketball games when they come to North Texas.

My wife was a school counselor for many years in North Carolina and a number of her former students were then attending UNCC, and my wife spent a frantic day trying to make contact with them to find out if they were safe.

Most mass shootings end when the second gunman arrives. Usually armed law enforcement, but sometimes it's an armed citizen. In this case, it was neither.

It was Riley Howell, an ROTC cadet from the Asheville area in western North Carolina, not far from where I grew up. Just up the mountain toward the Tennessee line.

Howell did not have a gun. At age 21 he was old enough to own one, but the UNCC campus, like most campuses in North Carolina, is a "gun-free" zone.

The question of "gun-free" zones is something we can debate (and have debated many times) elsewhere. Today I want to talk about the will to fight back and love of neighbor.

When Christ was asked by His disciples which was the most important commandment, He didn't pick one of the ten. He summarized them all. The most important, He said, summarizing the first three, is to love the Lord your God with all your heart, mind, soul, and strength.

The other, He said, summarizing the last seven, love your neighbor as yourself. The greatest commandment is love. Love of God and love of neighbor.[14]

The lack of a gun did not stop young Riley Howell. Guns are helpful, for sure. But the most important thing is the will to fight and the love of your neighbor as you love yourself.

With a gunman in his classroom and nowhere to hide, Howell charged the man and subdued him, ending the killing spree before more could be harmed. But in the process, Riley Howell lost his own life in service to his neighbor.

> *"Greater love has no one than this, that someone lay down his life for his friends."*[15]

---

[14] See Matthew 22:36-40 and Mark 12:28-31

[15] John 15:13

Before you utter that hackneyed phrase about good guys with guns, remember the life and sacrifice of Riley Howell.

FATHER'S DAY 2019

Father's Day dates back to the Middle Ages with the Feast of Saint Joseph, the earthly father of Christ. That feast day is still celebrated in the Roman Catholic tradition on March 19.

Father's Day did not make its way into general observance outside the Catholic tradition until the 20th century when it became a civic celebration to complement Mothers Day.

It started at a Methodist church in West Virginia in 1908, following a tragic mining accident that claimed the lives of 361 miners — 250 of whom left behind nearly 1000 children. That event never grew beyond that congregation, though.

Attempts were made to establish a celebration in other places: Chicago, Washington state, Oregon. None of them caught on.

In 1913, a bill was proposed to create a national holiday. President Woodrow Wilson spoke at a Father's Day celebration in 1916 and offered his support for the idea, but Congress resisted.

President Coolidge said the day should be observed throughout the nation in 1924, but didn't issue a proclamation that would have made it a national holiday.

At that point, the idea has lost steam.

In the 1930s Sonora Smart Dodd, returning to Spokane, Washington from her studies in Chicago, began to promote the idea of a celebration of fatherhood. She got the help of manufacturers of products traditionally geared toward men — ties, tobacco, pipes — and by 1938 she was teaming up with a major menswear retailers association to promote the idea nationwide.

It wasn't until 1957 that Maine Senator Margaret Chase Smith wrote a proposal to create Father's Day as an official, national holiday. Nine years later, President Lyndon Johnson issued a proclamation establishing the third Sunday in June as Father's Day.

64 years after that tragic West Virginia mine accident, President Nixon made it official in 1972 by signing Johnson's proclamation into law.

Given today's grievance culture, this next bit of info may be enough to get Father's Day revoked. Who was Sonora Smart Dodd, the woman who fought for the creation of fathers day in the 1920s and 1930s? She was the daughter of a confederate veteran who raised Dodd and her five siblings on his own.

So, thanks to the efforts of people like Sonora Smart Dodd, a Daughter of the Confederacy, we now have a day to celebrate fathers.

So, again I ask, what's the big deal about fathers?

The Fourth Commandment is the one commandment that comes with a promise.

> *"Honor your father and your mother, that your days will be long in the land that the Lord is giving you."*

Martin Luther wrote that there is no greater authority on earth than the authority of father and mother.

To paraphrase Luther, "to the estate of fatherhood and motherhood God has given the distinction above all lower estates that he commands us not only to love our parents but also to honor them. In this way, he sets fathers and mothers apart and distinguishes them above all other persons on earth."[16]

Proverbs 15 says that a fool despises his father's instruction,[17] and Proverbs 23 counsels children to listen to their fathers.[18]

But in America, it's increasingly difficult for children to honor their fathers or to receive proper instruction from them. Over 80% of single-parent families are headed by single mothers. 50% of those women were never married in the first place.

Almost two-thirds of minority children are born out of wedlock, and one-fourth of *all* children grow up without a father.

In the nearly 50 years since the official creation of Father's Day, the sexual revolution, radical feminism, and the media have told us that fathers don't really matter. Families come in all shapes, they say. Two mommies. Two daddies. No daddy.

---

[16] Martin Luther, The Large Catechism, 103-106

[17] Proverbs 15:5

[18] Proverbs 23:22

Rent-a-daddy. Whatever floats your boat.

So, why does Father's Day matter?

First, consider these sobering stats: 26% of those unmarried moms were jobless for the entire year in 2018. Despite making up less than 15% of the population, blacks account for one-third of all single-mother households. And while just six percent of married households are living in poverty, 39% of

single-mother families are poor.[19]

Kids growing up in single-parent families are almost three times as likely to be arrested than are kids in intact families. They are more than twice as likely to have committed assault.

Based on data from the U.S. Census Bureau, the Centers for Disease Control and Prevention, and the National Archive of Criminal Justice Data, studies have found that the top three factors that correlate most strongly with gun homicides are growing up in a black community, dropping out of high school, not having a father present.

---

[19] https://singlemotherguide.com/single-mother-statistics/

According to the National Fatherhood Initiative, nearly two-thirds (64 percent) of African American children are raised in homes without their biological fathers present, compared to 33 percent of *all* children in America.[20]

We have gone from "Father Knows Best" to "Fathers don't matter" in a span of 50 years.

Every weekend we see violence in cities like Chicago. Cities with strong gun laws, high poverty rates for African Americans, and high rates of single-parent families.

A significant percentage of the perpetrators of the nation's deadliest mass killings were raised in broken homes.

Luther wrote that when father and mother can no longer exercise control, either because the government has assumed the role of the parent or the parents are not present or are unwilling to exercise what he calls their "natural dominion over them," the hangman must take over.

"Where do so many rogues come from that must be daily hanged, beheaded, and broken upon the wheel?" Luther

---

[20] https://www.fatherhood.org/father-absence-statistic

wrote in the Large Catechism. "Don't they come from disobedience to parents, because they will not submit to discipline in kindness?"[21]

Modern, militant feminism tells us that fathers are unimportant. Masculine behavior is beaten out of our boys, derided and mocked as "toxic." With no father at home and a vast majority of females teaching in public schools, too many boys are raised with no positive male role models. No one to teach them positive masculine traits. Traits like bravery, standing up for the weak and protecting women.

I know. This is the world that I grew up in. I am the product of a single-parent family, a single mother family. I know the damage that is done to a child when their world falls apart. When the father leaves, and there's no one, not a man anyway, to guide you through those formative years.

It affects a young man for most of his life. To this day it affects me. I cannot look back fondly at memories with my Dad. I don't have words of wisdom passed down to me that I could lean on and learn from and pass on to my own children.

---

21 Martin Luther, The Large Catechism, 137

This is what the sexual revolution has brought us. Rather than men and women working together in complementary roles given to us by God: men now routinely walk away from their obligations. And millions of women are left to raise their offspring alone. Or worse, they abort the unborn child. The sexual revolution has also taught us that if the child is an inconvenience, or if it would be born into poverty or hardship, it would be better off dead.

Children, lacking guidance from their father, turn to other father-figures. They turn to drugs, alcohol, crime, depression, suicide, and in some cases mass murder.

What's the big deal about fathers? Why do we celebrate Father's Day?

Fathers are the rock of the family. The providers. The protectors and defenders. The teachers. The examples that children, young men especially, learn from and follow. Without their guidance and care, we can see the results, even if this corrupt world refuses to look: poverty, depression, death.

As our Heavenly Father, our earthly fathers "strengthen, confirm, nourish, and favor us." This is why Father's Day is more important than ever. As the role of fathers is diminished in society, their importance grows even greater.

To all faithful fathers in our audience, from everyone here at Armed Lutheran Radio, we thank you. And we wish you a very happy Father's Day.

WARNING SIGNS

Joe Biden, Beto O'Rourke, Elizabeth Warren, and a bevy of Democrat presidential hopefuls, have at various times voiced support for gun bans and the confiscation of "assault weapons," and then in the next breath said it would be a voluntary buyback. They proposed a federal law raising the age limit to own a gun to 21, expanding background checks, cracking down on gun dealers, making CEOs of gun companies personally liable for gun deaths, and doubling or tripling the taxes on gun and ammo purchases.

None of those ideas will have any effect on gun deaths. They will put people out of work, set the insane precedent that the owners of companies can be held responsible for the criminal misuse of their products, make it impossible to gift or loan guns to family or friends, and make it exceptionally expensive to afford ammo to train, compete, and hunt. As an added bonus, it will make the ownership of guns for home defense even more difficult for low-income Americans who live in crime-ridden inner cities.

They want to make gun and ammunition manufacturing and ownership so expensive that those industries eventually go away, eliminating by attrition, lawful civilian ownership of firearms.

Guess who doesn't care about the cost of the guns and ammo they steal? Guess who doesn't go through a background check to get a gun? Guess who doesn't get sued when they kill someone with a gun? Guess who won't be stopped by these ideas? Criminals. Criminals who don't obey the myriad of gun laws we already have but rarely enforce.

Saying that we have to "do something" is not enough. Cliches about mental illness or about how gun control doesn't work are not enough. There are no easy solutions, just as there is no single cause. As we have discussed before, the problem is sin, mental illness, and changes in society. Decades of moral decay and the unending effort to turn our system of values on its head cannot be undone quickly. If ever.

Politicians don't want difficult decisions. They don't want long processes. They want quick, cheap "fixes" that they can campaign on.

While there are no easy solutions there are steps that can be taken to reduce the risks and to identify threats before they become tragedies. Many of those steps involve re-examining laws that protect privacy while unintentionally making it harder to identify and act on the red flags that are always there.

In every case, there were warning signs that someone — sometimes lots of someones — saw. Parents, teachers, counselors, classmates. After 9/11 we talked about "See something, say something," but laws like HIPAA, FERPA, and laws protecting juvenile crime records hinder efforts to do just that. And there's also a reluctance on the part of many to get involved. And sometimes, like in Parkland, Florida, people tried to say something but nothing was done.[22]

Perhaps we should fix those issues before we turn the due process upside down or violate the rights of millions of Americans. Let us pray for the victims and their families, and for our politicians that they may make wise decisions, rather than rushing to do something to score political points.

---

[22] https://www.miamiherald.com/news/local/education/article221609300.html

THE SIN PROBLEM

A news story out of Japan caught my eye and I thought it was instructive. The Associated Press reports:

"A man screaming "You die!" burst into an animation studio in Kyoto, doused it with a flammable liquid and set it on fire Thursday, killing 33 people in an attack that shocked the country and brought an outpouring of grief from anime fans.

Thirty-six others were injured, some of them critically, in a blaze that sent people scrambling up the stairs toward the roof in a desperate — and futile — attempt to escape what proved to be Japan's deadliest fire in nearly two decades.

…

Police gave no details on the motive…

Japanese media reported the fire might have been set near the front door, forcing people to find other ways out.

…

Firefighters found 33 bodies, 20 of them on the third floor, and some on the stairs to the roof, where they had apparently collapsed…"[23]

What can we learn from this?

Well, before we get to the theological, let's look at what happened here and channel our inner Aaron Israel.[24]

The fire was set near the front door, forcing employees to find alternate exits. Which none of them did.

Where you work, do you know how to get out in an emergency? Is there an alternate exit you can get to if there's a fire or a gunman or some other obstacle keeping you from getting to the front door?

------

[23] https://apnews.com/article/b10907eaf37945889d9ee4339df92aaa

[24] Aaron Israel was a contributor to Armed Lutheran Radio from March 2016 to September of 2018. In many of his "Self-Defense Tip of the Week" segments, Aaron would review a news story and share lessons to improve your own personal security.

One lesson for us here is to have an emergency plan, practice it, walk through it so that if you have to get out of your workplace in a hurry, and the front door is blocked, you can get out some other way.

How do you practice your escape plan at work? Simple. Walk it when you go to lunch or when you leave work for the day. Rather than simply packing up and heading for your usual exit every day, take a different route several times a week so you memorize the path. Sure, it may mean some extra walking, but who can't use a little more of that? Am I right?

The other lesson is a broader one and more obvious. Here we have a mass killing in an Asian country where guns are banned and no guns were needed. You don't need a gun if you are really determined to cause mayhem.

We have talked about this many times on the podcast. About how the anti-gun Left tries to use mass shootings in America — school shootings in particular — as proof that there is something wrong with America. They claim that somehow this kind of violence is unique to us as a nation.

That claim is a lie. Mass shootings are not unique to the United States. But if you point that out they pivot to ignoring the facts and claiming that what is wrong with us is that we have too many guns. They compare our gun homicides to other countries, like Japan, to try to make the case for how horrible guns are and how we need gun control.

The problem, however, is not the gun, it is sin. A gun is just a tool. The determining factor in how it is used is what is in the heart of the person who uses it.

From Mark chapter 7 we read:

> *"What comes out of a person is what defiles him. For from within, out of the heart of man, come evil thoughts, sexual immorality, theft, murder, adultery, coveting, wickedness, deceit, sensuality, envy, slander, pride, foolishness. All these evil things come from within, and they defile a person."*[25]

---

[25] Mark 7:20-23

It wasn't the matches or the flammable liquid that caused that terrible tragedy in Tokyo. It was the wickedness in the heart of the arsonist. It was sin. That sin will drive some to commit terrible acts against their fellow men, and it doesn't matter if there's a gun available or not.

You might think this is a statistical outlier for a country like Japan. According to the story, however:

> *"The death toll exceeded that of a 2016 attack by a man who stabbed and killed 19 people at a nursing home in Tokyo."*

Once again, an Asian country and an Asian killer. No guns. 19 people dead. Not because of knives. Taking away pointy knives — as they do in the UK — won't stop people from killing. The problem is not the knife. Or the fire. Or the gun.

BABY MONICA

In my first book, *Here I Blog*, I have a chapter called "The Way Back to the Narrow Gate." In that chapter, I wrote about the difficult task of saving the culture. I wrote about the need to promote a culture of life. I thought about that chapter when this story out of Brooklyn, New York, caught my eye:

> "*A fetus that was discarded on a Brooklyn street has been given a name and received a proper funeral and burial... with police officers joining in the final tribute.*
>
> *Six NYPD officers acted as pallbearers at the service for baby Monica...An NYPD piper played dolefully.*
>
> *...*
>
> *Baby Monica was found dead under a tree near the Nathaniel Greene School in East New York... She was inside a bag surrounded by bloody clothing...The city Medical Examiner estimated that the fetus was about 20-weeks old and would not have been viable outside the womb.*

...

The Life Center of New York offered to provide a funeral for the fetus, named Monica after the mother of Saint Augustine

...

Baby Monica was buried in the Guardian Angel section of Resurrection Cemetery in Staten Island, which provides burial space for abandoned babies."[26]

First, kudos to the New York Police Department for their participation in this funeral. I'm not surprised that cops would participate, but I *am* surprised they were allowed to participate despite the fact that the city is run by a lunatic Leftist who supports abortion on demand with no limits.

This was reported by the New York Daily News, the Washington Times, and Lifesite News. It also got a surprising, but extremely short, mention in the Associated Press. Reuters, the New York Times, the Washington Post, the major news

---

[26] https://www.nydailynews.com/new-york/brooklyn/ny-funeral-mass-burial-for-dead-human-fetus-brooklyn-20190629-c2yxhzyjuvelfph22qq7ftvbqm-story.html

networks did not cover it at all.

It was a poignant and beautiful service, but why is this important?

We are told that a child in the womb, especially one at 20 weeks, is not really a child. It is a choice. A parasite. Something to be discarded like an appendix or your tonsils. Just a clump of cells. Yet, here we see this clump of cells being treated with respect. Given a name, and buried. Mourned by people who have no idea who the mother is.

This is an encouraging sign. This took place in one of the boroughs of the largest city in a state whose governor and legislators once excitedly cheered the passage of a law legalizing the un-restricted abortion of unborn children older than Baby Monica.

Too often our culture celebrates death. It cheapens life at all stages. Grandpa is getting old and it is too hard to take care of him and he is becoming a financial burden so we must euthanize him. Someone wears a hat that offends us, so we need to punch him.

A member of Congress disagrees with our political opinions, so we take a rifle to a baseball field and begin shooting. We disagree with the views of a speaker at our local college so we protest and prevent people from attending. Cops shoot a criminal so we riot and loot.

We celebrate movies where the protagonists solve their problems with guns and killing. We call the unborn child a burden if the mother isn't ready to have a child, so we tell her it's her choice. It is between her and her doctor to decide what's best for *her*. The child doesn't enter into it. We kill each other over sneakers. Kids, craving attention and angry because they are rejected by their classmates, seek to make a name for themselves by shooting up their school.

In short, we live in a culture that does not value life.

Jesus told his disciples:

> *"Enter by the narrow gate. For the gate is wide and the way is easy that leads to destruction, and those who enter by it are many. For the gate is narrow and the way is hard that*

Solving our problems with anger and violence and killing is easy. It is the wide way that we take all too often.

The narrow gate is tough to get through. Sacrificing to care for an elderly parent. Accepting (or at least tolerating) different political opinions or points of view. Turning the

other cheek to those who insult you. Waiting for all the facts after a police shooting. Working hard to save for the things we want and delaying gratification. Giving birth to a child when you're not stable financially and working hard to provide it a happy and healthy life. Or, giving a child up for adoption rather than killing it. Accepting that not everyone is going to like you.

It is tough. But we have to do it. We have to encourage it.

We went to the moon, for crying out loud. We are Americans. We don't take the easy road. We make things happen. We roll up our sleeves to do the dirty work. We never back down from a difficult road.

---

[27] Matthew 7:13-14

We need to celebrate and encourage that spirit again.

This funeral for Baby Monica may not seem like much, but it's important. It says that in this hedonistic society that has rejected God and morality at every turn, there are those — even in the heart of one of our most liberal cities — who still value life.

May God have mercy on baby Monica. And her mother. And may he grant that we, as a nation would turn from our

wicked ways and once again cherish the amazing gift of life that he has given us.

RED FLAGS

In the wake of two mass shootings, one in El Paso, Texas, and another within 24 hours in Dayton, Ohio, there was much discussion about what can we do that would help us prevent future shootings. Every single one of America's mass shooters had warning signs, "red flags" if you will. Signs that something was wrong and that was either ignored or rationalized or excused.

We don't need new gun control laws. Especially ones that don't address the real issues underlying mass violence. Background checks and "red flag" laws and various product bans would not have stopped either killer or any of the previous mass killers.

I have often talked about how technology connects us like never before, and yet we are more disconnected from our neighbors than ever. What we need is an engaged society. One that gets their noses out of their cellphones, pays attention and speaks up when something isn't right.

To stop these killers we need people to say something. We then need authorities to *do* something. Too often one or the other of those things just doesn't happen. Or both.

And, here's proof that this works without changing our gun laws or infringing on due process.

According to CNN, in the week following the shootings in El Paso and Dayton, 27 people were arrested for making similar violent threats across the nation.

In Long Beach California, police arrested a hotel worker whose fellow employee tipped off police that the guy was planning a shooting spree at the hotel. In Florida, a 15-year-old was detained after he made a threat to bring a gun to his school. In nine cases the targets were schools. In at least five cases the target was a Wal-Mart, as the attack in El Paso.

In each case, people spoke up and tragedies were averted. In a story at CNN.com, Madeline Holcombe wrote "If you see a red flag for a mass shooting, this is what you should do."[28]

---

[28] https://www.cnn.com/2019/08/18/us/mass-shooting-tips-what-to-do/index.html

I want to applaud Ms. Holcombe, because not once in that article does she advocate (or quote someone who advocates) for gun control laws. She advocates instead for speaking up and warning others if you believe there is a serious threat.

Whether it's the mother who is concerned about her son's

weapons or the woman whose boyfriend told her he had an urge to hurt others. Sometimes the people involved report their concerns to authorities, but more often — according to former FBI executive Katherine Schweit — they do not.

People talk themselves out of reporting, or even believing, red flags for various reasons. They fear being wrong, they are reluctant to involve the police, or they just don't want to get involved in other peoples' business.

To report suspicious behavior, one has to know what to look for -- and it's not a profile, a religion, a race, or diagnosis, Schweit said. Observable, unusual behaviors. Those closest to people who may commit violence know what behaviors are "unusual" for that individual.

Mass shootings are planned attacks. These shooters don't get out of bed one morning and decide to go shoot up Wal-Mart. They plan. They think about it. They may talk about it to others in person or online.

Maybe your co-worker is like the guy in Las Vegas who never really cared about guns, then one day he's got a dozen. A buying spree at a gun shop is not a crime, but combined with other factors it could be a warning sign.

Schweit says when it comes to preventing incidents of mass violence, community involvement is key.

Community involvement. Not new laws. Not gun confiscation. Just saying something when you see something. In the examples I mentioned here, without a single new law, almost thirty potential killers were thwarted.

Were they all serious threats? We don't know. Probably not. But I have no doubt that one or more of those thirty individuals would have attempted something like El Paso or Parkland. In the wake of a high profile mass shooting, copycats abound.

In the end, even if it turns out to be nothing, I'd rather inconvenience the stupid kid who jokes about mass shootings than lose my civil rights because Americans cannot be bothered to get involved.

And speaking up when you suspect something, that's part of being a good Christian.

The Christian life is not "live and let live." It is not navel-gazing and contemplating your relationship with God. It is bigger than you. It is loving your neighbor. Your warning

may help God's ordained authorities to protect your neighbors from harm.

As Martin Luther wrote in his explanation of the Fifth Commandment, to do nothing when you could defend your neighbor is the same as killing them yourself.[29] Think about that. We often hear people who knew the killer say something like "You know, I knew one day that guy was going to snap." If they know *before* the killings but didn't bother to say something, they have to live with the knowledge that they

---

[29] Martin Luther, The Large Catechism, 191-192

could have done something but didn't. Some amount of blood is on their hands.

Murder is not new. It is been with us since the dawn of man. We don't need new laws to stop the descendants of Cain. We need an engaged and active public to get their heads out of their asses and look out for their neighbors.

FROM ADVENT TO CHRISTMAS

Every year, once Thanksgiving is behind us, everyone in the world is in a rush to get to Christmas. Christmas music on the radio and Christmas decorations going up even before Thanksgiving has even arrived.

I prefer one holiday at a time, thank you. You put out the Halloween decorations in October, take them down and switch to Thanksgiving, then, when thanksgiving is finally done, you transition to Christmas. One at a time.

Every year it seems this fallen world is in a hurry to push us from one holiday to the next. One big sales event to another. But there's another season that is overlooked in this increasingly secular age: The beginning of the new church year and the season of Advent.

Advent leads us to Christmas. The Christmas season actually starts on Christmas day. The 12 days of Christmas do not lead up to that blessed day, they proceed from it.

But in this increasingly secular world of sales and shopping, and empty holidays of materialism, the Christmas season begins the day after Thanksgiving on "Black Friday."

I'm not suggesting that there's anything wrong with Christmas shopping or giving gifts. The giving of gifts to our loved-ones symbolizes the gift of a savior that God gives to us on Christmas Day.

But if you go to the Googles and search for "Black Friday mob" you will see what I am talking about. It's not the buying or the shopping that is the issue. It's what's in our hearts when we do it.

We spend a day giving thanks for our blessings. For all the wonderful things in our lives. The gifts that God has bestowed upon us. And then we follow that up with a mad dash to save 100 bucks on a new appliance or electronic thing-a-mabob to replace one we already have.

Many of the same people who decry corporate greed will stand in line for hours for the next gadget that is marginally better than the one they bought last year and which they already consider obsolete.

Some call this the "evil of capitalism." In truth, it's not capitalism that is the problem. It's mankind. The same greed and envy that killed Abel still lives in our hearts and makes itself known in varying ways and to various degrees.

So, as we pass on from Thanksgiving and the materialism of Black Friday and the Christmas shopping season keep in mind that it's still not Christmas yet.

Despite the decorations and the lights and the music, it's Advent, a season of watching and hopefulness. A season of looking forward to and preparing for Christ's coming.

The reason you do not hear about the big "Advent sales event" on TV is that our modern sensibilities — and the Old Adam — are not so much interested in the season of Advent. Like the season of Lent, the fallen world prefers to skip straight to the good stuff and past all that reflective and penitential stuff.

The idea that we are looking forward to the birth of a Savior — and ultimately to his return at judgment day and the end of this wicked world — doesn't play well in the sale papers. "Buy now before christ returns!" doesn't really sell a lot of flat screens.

Our world is increasingly hostile to God's Word and to those who cling to it. Especially those of us who consider God's Word to be without error and those of us who refuse to change God's Word to fit modern mores.

Too many Christians prefer the feel-good parts of Christianity. Openly gay, pro-abortion, anti-gun. People who think that the Bible is to be interpreted by each of us based on modern standards rather than God's eternal standards. Or the prosperity gospel hucksters who use the gospel to get rich by selling the idea that your salvation is in your hands. All you have to do is think positive thoughts.

They are wolves in the skins of sheep, leading millions of

souls to their eternal damnation while preaching a false gospel of social justice and works righteousness.

We live in a time of growing darkness, where perversion and decadence are celebrated, paganism is admired and Christian values of family and faith are demonized. The Ten Commandments are ignored and trashed as outdated, bigoted, misogynistic.

But during Advent, we look forward to the light that will drive away that darkness. The light of the world that came

into our flesh, dwelt among us and died for the forgiveness of our sins. The sins of idolatry. The sins of envy and hatred. The sins of sexual immorality and false speech.

We look forward to Christ's return when he will come again in glory to judge this world and establish his eternal kingdom. When the wheat will be separated from the chaff and all evil will be swept away into the fires of damnation.

That doesn't really work well in the sale papers and the TV ads. It's a little too much for our degenerate world to celebrate.

"It's still not Christmas," wrote Dietrich Bonhoeffer in a letter to his parents in 1943. "But it's also still not the great last Advent…[T]he advent season is a season of waiting, but our whole life is an Advent season, that is a season of waiting for the last advent, for the time when there will be a new heaven and a new earth…We can and we should celebrate Christmas despite the ruins around us…We must do all this even more intensively because we do not know how much longer we have."[30]

---

[30] Dietrich Bonhoeffer, *God is in the Manger*, (John Knox Press, 2010), 2-3

THE CHRISTMAS TRUCE

On Christmas Day we begin the season of joy as we celebrate the gift of a Savior, sent to redeem us, to die for us, and to unite mankind to him and reclaim us from our sin, from death and the devil.

On Christmas Day in 1914 young Henry Williamson was a private in the London Rifle Brigade. He was manning a trench in Belgium following the First Battle of Ypres which had pulverized 95,000 British soldiers in three months at the dawn of modern, industrial warfare.

Twenty-three years later, looking out over the starlit grasses outside his English home, he wrote this account of his memories from that night in the freezing cold of the Ypres salient.[31]

---

[31] Williamson's account of the Christmas Truce was published in the *London Daily Express* on Christmas Eve in 1937. You can find the full text here: https://www.henrywilliamson.co.uk/first-world-war/57-uncategorised/158-henry-williamson-and-the-christmas-truce

Williamson was enduring the bitter cold that night. Their 7" overcoats were stiff as boards, our boots were too hard to remove, but we rejoiced."

They rejoiced at the prospect of a good night's sleep inside. In a newly constructed blockhouse that they called the "Piccadilly Hotel."

"No bed but the cold earth, no blankets even; but sleep. Sleep!"

But their hopes were dashed by the arrival of a message from headquarters calling for wiring parties in "No Man's Land" all night. Worse yet, there would be a bright moon.

In the days before wireless communication, networks of telephone wires crisscrossed the Great War's battlefields. These were frequently cut by shelling and enemy sabotage. Wiring parties were required to sneak into the battlefield between the two lines of trenches — "No Man's Land" — to re-connect or re-string the wires. A cloudless night and a bright moon would make their work more dangerous as they crept only fifty yards from the German lines.

"The moon was high and white among frozen cloudlets. We were visible. Someone slipped, with a clank of spade or rifle. We flung ourselves on our faces. We waited. The battlefield was as silent as the moon."

But then at midnight, they heard laughing and singing from the German lines. They sang Christmas carols. Soon a Christmas tree, lighted with candles appeared on the parapet of the trench.

There were shouts in English: "Come on over, Tommy! We won't shoot you."[32] And then a dark figure approached and Williamson haltingly walked toward it, fearing a trap.

"Merry Christmas, English friend!" They shook hands.

"Then I saw that the light on the pole was the morning star, the Star in the East. It was Christmas morning."

All that day English and German soldiers mingled and talked No Man's Land. Both sides worked to bury their dead in shallow graves. Crosses were set to mark them made from

---

[32] British soldiers came to be known as "Tommy" in reference to a poem by Rudyard Kipling called *Barrack Room Ballards*, written in 1892.

ration-box wood.

They wrote on the crosses "For King and Country."

In German *"Für Vaterland und Freiheit."*

Fatherland and Freedom.

"Freedom? How was this? We were fighting for freedom!"

Then Williamson came to a stunning thought. Both sides believed that what they were fighting for was right. They were fighting for the same thing.

"The war was a terrible mistake! People at home did not know this!" If they did, he thought, the war would quickly be over.

"These fellows in grey were good fellows, they were – strangely – just men like ourselves."

In the midst of that misery, the combatants in that colossal struggle found a way to see the humanity in the men in the other trench. Men, whom their leaders told them they should hate.

One hundred and six years later, here "across the Pond," our nation is divided like never before. Left from right. Liberal from conservative. Men vs. women. Rich vs. poor. White vs. black. Political elites vs. the common citizen.

Our leaders tell us that those who disagree with us are not people. They are "enemies." They are evil. If you know your history — and most Americans do not — that attitude, taken to the extreme, has lead to misery and human suffering, and mass death over the past century.

Lord, help us to see the humanity in our fellow Americans. Give us the ability to see through the lies that our leaders, on all sides of the various political divides, want us to hear.

Lord, give us the courage to question our own political beliefs. to listen to those ideas and opinions with which we disagree.

And no matter how bitter the divides become, Lord help us to always recognize that those on the opposite side are human beings. Your children. Created in your image.

During this and every succeeding joyous season of Christmas, help us to remember that you sent your Son, Jesus Christ, to die for our sins. All of our sins. Even the sins of those who oppose us. Even those who refuse to recognize their own sins. Even those who refuse to recognize you or your son.

In Jesus' Holy Name we pray.

Amen and Merry Christmas.

ABOUT THE AUTHOR

Born in New York City and raised in North Carolina, Lloyd Bailey Jr. but didn't become a "gun guy" until later in life. He wanted to know how he, as a Christian, should think about gun rights. That led to the Armed Lutheran blog in 2012 and the Armed Lutheran Radio podcast in 2016.

Armed Lutheran Radio Year Four is his sixth book and the fourth in the Armed Lutheran Radio series.

Today, he lives in Texas with his wife and two children. He writes software, thinks about theology, hosts podcasts, and is a competitive shooter.

OTHER ARMED LUTHERAN BOOKS

Bailey, Lloyd, et al; *"Duty to Defend,"* 2020. Print, eBook.

Bailey, Lloyd; *"Armed Lutheran Radio: Year Three,"* 2019. Print, eBook.

Bailey, Lloyd; *"Armed Lutheran Radio: Year Two,"* 2019. Print, eBook.

Bailey, Lloyd; *"Armed Lutheran Radio: Year One,"* 2019. Print, eBook.

Bailey, Lloyd; *"Here I Blog."* **Third Edition**, 2019. Print, eBook.

Bailey, Lloyd; *"Starting a Church Shooting Club,"* 2018. eBook.